Who Was Lucille Ball?

by Pam Pollack and Meg Belviso

illustrated by Gregory Copeland

Penguin Workshop

Perfect Perles—Wendy Perle Van Deusen and
Juliet Perle Van Deusen—PP

To Sunflower and Marigold,
a couple of red-headed screwballs—MB

PENGUIN WORKSHOP
An Imprint of Penguin Random House LLC, New York

Text copyright © 2017 by Pam Pollack and Meg Belviso.
Illustrations copyright © 2017 by Penguin Random House LLC. All rights reserved.
Published by Penguin Workshop, an imprint of Penguin Random House LLC, New York.
PENGUIN and PENGUIN WORKSHOP are trademarks of Penguin Books Ltd.
WHO HQ & Design is a registered trademark of Penguin Random House LLC.
Printed in the USA.

Visit us online at www.penguinrandomhouse.com.

Library of Congress Control Number: 2017935683

ISBN 9780448483030

10 9

Contents

Who Was Lucille Ball?

In the spring of 1952, cities across America experienced a mysterious drop in the water pressure every week between 9:30 and 9:35 p.m. In New York City, it seemed impossible to get a taxi on a Monday night. All the cabbies were off duty. And in Chicago, a department store changed its business hours because it seemed like no one was shopping on Monday nights anymore.

What was going on?

It turned out that it was all related to a TV show! A half-hour comedy.

On Monday nights, Americans from coast to coast rushed through their dinner. Kids finished their homework as fast as they could.

By nine o'clock everyone gathered in front of their televisions. And waited. In the 1950s, TVs took a while to warm up. Finally a big heart appeared against a satin background. The theme song of *I Love Lucy* began, and America was watching. It turned out that the viewers across the country were all waiting for the show to be over before using the bathroom.

Toilets all flushing at the same time had caused the water pressure to drop throughout one city! No one wanted to miss a minute of Lucy.

Lucille Ball, the star of the show, was the most beloved woman on television. Whatever trouble she was in, Lucy could make it seem like the funniest thing anyone had ever seen. All over the country, people couldn't stop laughing.

How did Lucille Ball become one of America's first big TV stars? It wasn't easy. She worked for years in Hollywood, making movies before she got a chance to show TV viewers how funny she could be. But she wasn't afraid of hard work.

And she wasn't afraid to take a pie in the face or fill her pockets with eggs or her mouth with chocolates, all to make people laugh. *I Love Lucy* was the name of her show, and how could you not?

CHAPTER 1
Lucyball

Lucille Desiree Ball was born in Jamestown, New York, on August 6, 1911. Although she always preferred Lucille, her family nicknamed her Lucyball, and the world came to know and love her as Lucy. Her father, Henry, worked for Bell Telephone, putting up phone lines all over the country, so he, Lucy, and Lucy's mother, Desiree, moved around a lot.

When Lucy was three and her mother was pregnant, Henry died of typhoid fever. Lucy and her mother, who was known as "DeDe," moved in with DeDe's parents, Frederick and Florabelle Hunt. The family lived in Celoron, New York, not far from Jamestown. There, Lucy's brother, Fred Ball, was born in 1915.

Other relatives came to live at the house in Celoron, too, including Lucy's young cousin Cleo.

Grandpa Fred took Lucy to the theater to see the live vaudeville shows in Jamestown on Saturdays and to the silent "flickers" (movies) shown outside in the park during the summer months.

Vaudeville

From the 1880s through the 1930s, the most popular form of live entertainment in the United States was vaudeville. Each show was made up of many different performers. The stage acts might include singers, dancers, jugglers, acrobats, or even trained animals. Some of the most popular performers were also the funniest. Favorite comedians, like Buster Keaton and Charlie Chaplin, started out in vaudeville and went on to become stars of early movies.

Even though she was still very young, Lucy was a responsible girl. After her grandmother died, she looked after her younger cousins. From the time she was ten, she took any odd job she could find. She sold hot dogs at the local boardwalk, and she worked at an ice-cream shop until she was fired for always forgetting to put the banana in the banana split.

By the time she was a teenager, Lucy was very independent. She was the first girl in town to bob—or cut short—her hair, which was very shocking in the early 1920s. She was a "flapper"— a slang word for the rebellious young women who wore makeup and short skirts.

Lucy liked it when people in town talked about her. She loved the attention. What she really wanted was to be onstage like the performers in the vaudeville acts or in the flickers. There weren't a lot of ways to become famous in Celoron. So Lucy started to think about where else she might follow her dream. New York City wasn't that far away. Many of the theaters in America were right there on Broadway.

Lucy had never really tried to act before. She couldn't sing or dance, but she thought she could learn. If she just worked hard enough, Lucy was sure she could become a star. And she had never been afraid of hard work.

By age fifteen, Lucy had convinced her mother to let her attend acting school in New York City. Even though money was tight, DeDe agreed to pay for Lucy to go for a six-week trial period. Lucy did her best at the school, but her teachers didn't think she had any talent. At the end of the six weeks, the school sent Lucy home with a note telling DeDe that she was wasting her money. They said Lucy would never be an actress.

But Lucy didn't care what the school thought. If they didn't want her, she would make it in New York on her own.

CHAPTER 2
Ain't Meant for Show Business

Over the next seven years, Lucy traveled back and forth between New York City and Celoron. She tried out for any acting job she could find, but she rarely got cast. Not even when she briefly changed her name to the more glamorous "Diane Belmont" and later simply to "Montana."

And then it seemed as if her luck was changing. Lucy got a job in a Broadway show. She would be in the chorus. That meant she was one of a dozen girls who sang and danced together behind the star of the show. But after only two rehearsals, the stage manager fired her. "It's no use, Montana," he told her. "Go home. You ain't meant for show business."

Lucy earned money selling makeup at drugstores and modeling in department stores. She tried on outfits for wealthy shoppers. If the customers liked how they looked on Lucy, they might try the clothes on themselves.

In the spring of 1933, she became a Chesterfield Girl, a model in the advertisements for Chesterfield cigarettes. Lucy was pictured in a skirt that showed off her long legs on billboards,

posters, and window displays. She often walked around town looking for her face on Chesterfield billboards. When she found one she would stand in front of it, hoping someone would recognize her. Nobody ever did. Lucy didn't yet have the eye-catching red hair she would later be famous for. She was just another blond girl on the crowded New York City sidewalks.

Lucy was now twenty-two. She had been trying to get work as an actress for seven years. She wondered if she would ever break into show business.

One morning as Lucy took a walk down Broadway, she bumped into Sylvia Hahlo. Sylvia was an agent. She hired a lot of pretty girls and dancers for New York nightclub shows and also for movies.

Sylvia was thrilled to run into Lucy. She had just hired a group of actresses to work at Goldwyn Studios in Hollywood. One of the young women had dropped out at the last minute, so Sylvia was looking to replace her. The girls were leaving on Saturday, and there was no time for a screen test. Would Lucy be willing to leave quickly for California?

Of course she would! Sylvia gave Lucy a coat, a hat, and a dress. She promised her that if the job with Samuel Goldwyn, the head of the studio, didn't work out, she could come back to New York. When Lucy boarded the Twentieth-Century Limited train at Grand Central Terminal at the end of the week, she was sure she had finally gotten her lucky break.

CHAPTER 3
Queen of the Bs

Samuel Goldwyn

When Lucy and the other young women from New York arrived in Hollywood, they were lined up, wearing bathing suits, by Samuel Goldwyn. He wanted to see if the actresses that Sylvia had sent from New York were pretty enough to be Hollywood stars. To make him laugh,

Lucy stuffed her bathing suit with anything she could find—toilet paper, gloves, and socks.

The joke did make Mr. Goldwyn laugh—and got her a screen test. After seeing the test,

Goldwyn wanted to send Lucy back to New York, but the director Busby Berkeley liked her. He gave her a part in a film he was making called *Roman Scandals*. Lucy didn't have any lines, but finally she was in a movie.

From the 1920s to the 1960s, the Hollywood movie industry operated under the "studio system." A small number of major studios made movies on their own lots—the property they owned in and around Los Angeles. Actors who signed contracts with a studio were paid a salary and did whatever work the studio had for them. The actors received steady paychecks, but the studio controlled their entire careers. Studio bosses "created" movie stars any way they thought would make money for their studios. They changed actors' names, set them up on dates, and made up stories about their past and present lives for the press.

Lucy was willing to do anything to stay in Hollywood. After *Roman Scandals* she had tiny parts in lots of movies. She took lessons at the studio, learning how to sing and dance, and how to do hair and makeup.

Lucy felt like she was back in acting school. She couldn't sing or dance as well as the other students could. She didn't think she was very pretty.

The only way she could get attention was by being a clown. She made faces, pretended to fall down, and made jokes. But none of it made Sam Goldwyn want to turn her into a big star.

Although her movie career seemed to be moving slowly, her personal life was not. She fell in love with a handsome young actor named George Raft. George introduced Lucy to his glamorous Hollywood friends. He took her to nightclubs and boxing matches in a fancy custom-built Cadillac.

He even had a bodyguard! But when Lucy introduced George to a friend of hers, he fell in love with her friend and out of love with Lucy.

Even so, Lucy and George remained friends. George helped Lucy get a contract at Columbia Pictures studio. She would be earning seventy-five dollars a week.

Now that she had a contract, Lucy brought her family from the East Coast out to California. DeDe, Fred, Grandpa, and Cleo all shared a small house above Sunset Boulevard, one of the most famous streets in Hollywood.

Screwball Comedies

During the 1930s, some of the most popular movies in America were "screwball comedies." They were usually about a couple who loved each other but often couldn't get along. They were known for their crazy plots, fast-paced jokes, and happy endings. Screwball humor was sometimes similar to the slapstick comedy that had been so popular in vaudeville. It often involved silly antics and not a lot of common sense.

Some of Hollywood's greatest actresses, including Katharine Hepburn, Carole Lombard, and Irene Dunne, were known for their screwball comedies. A few of the most popular were *My Man Godfrey*, *The Awful Truth*, *It Happened One Night*, *His Girl Friday*, and *Bringing Up Baby*.

In 1934, America was in the middle of the Great Depression. It was a time when many people lost their jobs and their life savings. Everyone was having trouble earning enough money. Even a big studio like Columbia Pictures needed to cut back. So Columbia began firing many of its actors. Lucy was out of work again.

A friend told her another studio, RKO, was looking for pretty actresses for a movie called *Roberta*. Lucy jumped at the chance. At RKO, Lucy started dating Pandro Berman, a young producer. Pandro cast her in a couple of films, including *Stage Door*, where she played a tough-talking chorus girl. Another actress in the film, Eve Arden, became a lifelong friend of Lucy's.

Eve Arden

The two of them always seemed to get the same kind of parts: the "drop-gag" girls. "You'd walk through a room, drop a smart remark, and exit," Lucy later explained. Lucy was good in these parts, and she got a lot of them, but they didn't make her a star.

In February 1935, Lucy's name appeared onscreen for the very first time in the credits for the

movie *Carnival*. Although she had been in fourteen other movies, her parts were so small and unimportant, her name wasn't mentioned in the cast. Before *Carnival*, most of the movies Lucy appeared in were not movies that everyone went to see. At that time, movies were shown as double features. The picture with the big movie stars was called the "A" picture, and it was shown first. Then they showed another, shorter film with less-famous actors. That was the "B" picture. Lucy made so many of these shorter movies, she became known as the "Queen of the Bs."

By 1940, Lucy was twenty-nine. She still couldn't sing or dance that well, but RKO cast her as a college freshman in the musical *Too Many Girls*. Her costar in the movie was a twenty-three-year-old Cuban band leader, Desi Arnaz. For Desi and Lucy, it was love at first sight.

Desi Arnaz

CHAPTER 4
Mr. and Mrs. Arnaz

Lucy and Desi met in June 1940 in the cafeteria—known as the commissary—at RKO studios. Desi was having lunch with director George Abbott. They talked about the movie Desi was going to be in called *Too Many Girls*.

When Lucy came into the commissary, she had a black eye. Her hair was hanging in her face. Her tight dress was torn. Desi was surprised when George said hello to her.

"What was that?" he asked when Lucy limped away on her broken high-heeled shoes.

"That's Lucille Ball," said George. "She's going to be in *Too Many Girls* with you."

Desi didn't know how he felt about this tough girl with a black eye being in his movie.

Later, while Desi was rehearsing at the studio, a girl walked in. Desi thought she was beautiful, with her big blue eyes and reddish-blond hair. He started singing just for her. He was shocked when he learned this mysterious woman was the same Lucille Ball he'd met at lunch! Lucy had simply been in costume for a different movie.

Desi asked her if she knew how to do the rumba, a Cuban dance.

"No, but I bet you do," she said.

Desi told her he could teach her the dance—but only if she went out with him that night. Lucy said yes. On November 30 of that same year, they got married.

Desi had grown up in the island country of Cuba. His father was the mayor of the city of Santiago. Desi planned to go to law school in the United States when he graduated from high school. But in 1933 his family moved to Miami, Florida, and Desi's life changed forever.

Desi, who had once lived like a prince, now earned money selling canaries and pottery while going to high school and learning to speak English.

In Cuba he had played the guitar for fun. Now he bought a secondhand guitar and got a job playing in a local hotel. The customers loved to dance to Desi's Cuban rumba beat. He was soon getting jobs with bands, and eventually he became the leader of a band of his own.

He decided what songs to play and directed the other musicians. That led to a job on Broadway, and then Hollywood. Desi was a bandleader onstage *and* in the movies.

Lucy and Desi bought a little ranch in the San Fernando Valley, about ten miles away from Hollywood. But since Desi's job took him around the country while Lucy worked in Hollywood, they didn't see much of each other.

Lucy and Desi wanted to find a way to spend more time together. In 1941 they created an act with songs that they could perform onstage together. But their dream was put on hold when America entered World War II.

Desi traveled around the country with other Hollywood stars, putting on shows to raise money for the war. He also performed at army bases for the soldiers. In 1942, Lucy signed a new contract with a yet another studio: MGM. She was cast in *Dubarry Was a Lady*, her first big role at MGM.

World War II

In 1939, Germany started invading neighboring countries. France and Great Britain soon declared war on Germany. America stayed out of the war until December 7, 1941, when Germany's ally Japan attacked a US military base, called Pearl Harbor, in Hawaii. America declared war and entered the fighting in Europe and in the Pacific. Men joined the army, navy, and air force. And women went to work to help the war effort. In Hollywood, many celebrities enlisted to fight. Others made movies and trips abroad to encourage the soldiers.

It was the first color film for Lucy. Up to this time, most Hollywood movies had been filmed in black-and-white. The hairstylist at Lucy's new studio dyed Lucy's blond hair "strawberry pink" so that it would stand out onscreen. Lucy decided to keep her hair that vivid red color for the rest of her life.

But her new hair color didn't make Lucy a star. She was still getting only small parts at MGM. Lucy had a lot of time to spend with a new friend she'd met at the studio, the silent film star Buster Keaton. Keaton's movies were still popular even though they had no sound. Lucy wanted to know how he managed to be so funny without ever saying a word.

Buster Keaton (1895–1966)

Buster Keaton started out in vaudeville, performing with his father. As part of the family comedy act, young Buster was thrown around, sometimes right off the stage! He wasn't hurt—it was all part of the act. After Buster learned to keep a straight face throughout the act, audiences laughed even harder. When he became famous as a star of silent movies, he was nicknamed "The Great Stone Face."

Buster Keaton is a comedy legend whose silent movies are still loved today.

Buster Keaton taught Lucy about the tricks he used onscreen. He showed her how to take a simple prop, like a lamp or a chair, and make a whole skit out of it. That kind of comedy wasn't really popular in Hollywood anymore. People loved to laugh at the clever jokes of the screwball comedies. But Lucy saw that Buster's style of comedy could still make people laugh.

Lucy made more movies with MGM, but none of them were big hits. Like Lucy, Desi also had a new contract with MGM. But he was drafted into the army in 1943 and sent to work at a hospital in California.

The hospital cared for a lot of wounded soldiers. Desi wasn't a doctor, but it was his job to make sure the patients kept their spirits up and kept busy.

After the war ended, Lucy accepted the lead role in a radio comedy show, *My Favorite Husband.* The show premiered in July 1948, and Lucy's role as a housewife got the attention of the people at the CBS network. They were interested in creating shows for the new sensation in American homes: the television. They hoped to turn the radio comedy into a TV show.

The Birth of Television

In the early 1950s, when television first became popular in the United States, there weren't many TV stations in operation. They were either on the East or West Coasts. But by 1955, half of all US households had TV sets. Many of the earliest programs were based on well-known radio shows and short films, like *The Adventures of Ellery Queen* and *Gangbusters*. But soon new shows were being created just for TV. As more stations were built all over the country, the price of TV sets became more affordable. By 1960, nine out of ten homes in the country had a television.

Lucy knew the perfect person to play her husband on television: her own husband, Desi Arnaz! But the producers at CBS didn't think viewers would believe that Lucy could be married to a man with a Cuban accent. They probably meant that people wouldn't like seeing a red-haired, blue-eyed actress like Lucy with a Hispanic husband. But Lucy wouldn't back down.

She decided to prove them wrong. She and Desi began rehearsing the act they had put together in the months before World War II. They practiced their funny routines and songs. They performed the show at movie theaters before the films started. Audiences loved them.

In the end, CBS decided to create a show about a marriage between a housewife—Lucy—and her famous Cuban bandleader husband. Lucy and Desi were thrilled. Not only were they going to be on television together, but also Lucy had just learned she was going to have a baby.

After years of hard work, and now in her late thirties, Lucy felt that she had finally gotten her big break. But with a baby on the way, she was going to be very busy!

CHAPTER 5
America Loves Lucy

Lucy and Desi's own company, Desilu Productions, was in charge of their new show. Lucy would play a New York housewife. Her husband, played by Desi, would be a bandleader in the city. Their show, called *I Love Lucy*, was a "situation comedy." That meant it was about characters who lived or worked together and

resolved a certain "situation"—that week's story—
by the end of each episode. Funny shows like this
became so popular they were often called by the
shorter name "sitcom."

In the new show, Lucy and Desi played Lucy
and Ricky Ricardo. They lived in an apartment
building in New York City. Their best friends
were their neighbors, Fred and Ethel Mertz.

Lucy Ricardo had dreams of being a star. She often tried to get herself into Ricky's nightclub shows. Many of the episodes had the two wives, Lucy and Ethel, competing against their husbands. Every episode showed Lucy getting herself into crazy situations that she often tried to resolve before her husband came home. Lucille Ball used all the tricks she learned from Buster Keaton to

be funny without talking.

Most TV shows at the time were done live. That meant people were watching the show at home as it was being performed in the studio. Viewers on the West Coast had to watch the program earlier because of the three-hour time difference between the two coasts. But, unlike other TV shows at the time, Lucy and Desi filmed their live shows the same way that movies were made. This is the reason that *I Love Lucy* can still be watched today.

While they were working on the new show, Lucy was getting closer and closer to having her baby. Her daughter, Lucie Desiree Arnaz, was born on July 17, 1951.

In honor of his new daughter, Desi wrote a song, "There's a Brand New Baby at Our House." Both Lucy and Desi went right back to work filming the show.

On Monday, October 15, 1951, the first episode of *I Love Lucy* aired on television.

By the spring of 1952, *I Love Lucy* was the highest rated show on TV. It was watched in ten million households each week. Strange things started happening in the United States on Monday nights. Everyone was waiting until *I Love Lucy* was over to use the bathroom, so all the toilets were flushing at once! In New York City it seemed impossible to get a taxi because all the cab drivers were taking breaks to watch the show in local bars.

By May 1952, the show was watched by more people than saw most Hollywood movies. Lucy had found her true home on television.

Lucy's Greatest Hits

Here are some of the most famous moments in *I Love Lucy* history.

"LUCY'S ITALIAN MOVIE"

Hoping to get a part in an Italian movie, Lucy volunteers to stomp grapes with her bare feet for an Italian wine-maker. While standing in the giant vat of grapes, she gets into a fight with another worker, making a complete grape-juice mess.

"JOB SWITCHING"

Lucy and Ethel get jobs in a candy factory wrapping chocolates on an assembly line. When they can't keep up with the speed of the conveyer belt, they try to hide the candy anywhere they can, including their mouths.

"LUCY DOES A TV COMMERCIAL"

Lucy films a commercial for a new health tonic, called Vitameatavegamin. Although it's made from vitamins, meat, vegetables, and minerals, it's really mostly alcohol.

The more she rehearses the commercial, the more she drinks. Although she is trying to sound peppy, by the end of the show she can barely speak.

"L.A. AT LAST!"

When Lucy sees one of her favorite movie stars at the famous Brown Derby Restaurant, she winds up getting tangled in her own plate of spaghetti and accidentally throwing a pie in his face.

"LUCY DOES THE TANGO"

Lucy decides to raise chickens and ends up hiding dozens of eggs in her clothing—right before Ricky suggests they practice the tango. Can Lucy keep the eggs in one piece while Ricky tries to hold her close? The episode ends with another Lucy mess. This episode got what many say is the longest laugh in TV history: sixty-five seconds! The laugh was so long it had to be shortened for TV.

CHAPTER 6
Little Ricky

Even after Lucy learned she was going to have another baby, she had no intention of taking time off from the *I Love Lucy* filming schedule. Lucy and Desi hoped to make Lucy's pregnancy part of the show by having the character of Lucy Ricardo be pregnant, too. But the television network thought that showing a pregnant woman was unsuitable for family viewing! They thought that Lucy's pregnancy should be kept secret. In the end, Lucy and Desi convinced them that Lucy's TV character should be pregnant, too. It was the first time a pregnancy was shown on television!

The episode of *I Love Lucy* called "Lucy Goes to the Hospital" aired on January 19, 1953.

It was said to have been watched by more viewers than the president's inauguration. The Ricardos' new baby—known as "Little Ricky"—became the most famous child in television history.

Earlier that same morning a crowd of reporters followed Desi into the hospital where the real Lucy was giving birth. When Desi learned he had a son, he ran out shouting to the reporters, "It's a boy! It's a boy! That's Lucy for you! Always does her best to cooperate! Now we have everything!" They named their son Desiderio Alberto Arnaz IV —Desi Arnaz Jr.

Lucy's Two Sons

When Lucille Ball had a baby boy, the Arnazes received 27,863 letters and cards, 3,154 telegrams, and 638 packages containing gifts for the baby. They had to hire four secretaries just to handle all that mail!

Lucy and little Desi Jr. appeared on the very first cover of *TV Guide* magazine, which may have confused many readers into thinking he played her TV son, Little Ricky. (He did not.) But the public didn't seem to care. They wanted to celebrate Lucy and Desi's baby with them. They rushed out to buy Little Ricky dolls, aprons, furniture, jewelry, and even potty seats that companies made in honor of Lucy's TV baby *and* her real son.

As far as America was concerned, Lucille Ball and Desi Arnaz *were* Lucy and Ricky Ricardo. America loved Lucy. But in the 1950s, some Americans lived in great fear of the spread of Communism, a type of society where all the land and businesses are owned by the government. Many US citizens, especially those who worked in radio, television, and movies, were accused of wanting to help make Communist ideas popular in the United States. Congress questioned them and sometimes banned them from working for years if they thought they were guilty.

In the 1930s, Lucy's beloved grandfather had encouraged her to join the Communist political party. During the Great Depression, Communism appealed to some working people. Lucy had  agreed to join, simply to please her grandfather.

Now angry congressmen were accusing her of being an enemy of the United States! In September 1953, Lucy was called to testify before the House Un-American Activities Committee (HUAC).

Lucy was afraid that people would turn against her. Desi was angry at the accusations and stood by his wife. And so did fans of *I Love Lucy*. When Lucy met privately with HUAC investigators, she was cleared of any wrongdoing or Communist connections. Her fans had remained loyal, and Lucy would always be grateful to them.

House Un-American Activities Committee

The US House of Representatives created the House Un-American Activities Committee (HUAC) in 1938. The committee feared that people working in Hollywood could influence Americans through movies and television shows to believe in Communism. They interviewed people and blacklisted—

banned from working—anyone who seemed to share or promote Communist ideas.

In 1969 HUAC redirected itself to focus on domestic terrorism. It was now called the House Internal Security Committee. Six years later, the House of Representatives abolished the committee.

Desi was still working very long hours running their company and producing *I Love Lucy*. But by 1957, Lucy and Desi seemed to get along better onscreen than off. At the end of a long day, Desi preferred to go to nightclubs, while Lucy stayed at home with their children in their new mansion in Beverly Hills.

Lucie and Desi Jr. knew better than anyone that the parents they watched on the *I Love Lucy* show were not the same parents they lived with. The characters of Lucy and Ricky Ricardo always made up by the end of the episode. Lucy and Desi Arnaz never stopped fighting.

That year, they filmed the last episode of *I Love Lucy*, which was already being shown in reruns. The income from the show had earned Lucy and Desi enough money to buy RKO studios—the same studio where they had met nearly twenty years earlier.

Now that the show was over, they wanted to work on the Arnaz family as hard as they had worked on being the Ricardos.

In May 1959, the family took a trip to Europe. But the trip didn't patch up the marriage. By the time they returned home, they were barely speaking. As much as Lucy wanted Desi to stay at home with the family, Desi always seemed to find other things to do.

Lucy and Desi decided to make occasional shows about the Ricardos, which were called *The Lucy-Desi Comedy Hour.*

The last one aired on March 2, 1960. In "Lucy Meets the Mustache," Lucy and Ricky Ricardo seemed as happy as ever. The very next day, the Arnazes announced that their marriage was ending. Lucy and Desi were getting a divorce. And *I Love Lucy* was officially over.

CHAPTER 7
Back to Broadway

What would Lucy do now? She decided to go back to New York. After all these years, she was finally going to be in a Broadway show. The musical was called *Wildcat*. Lucy would play Wildcat Jack, a woman who tricks a Western town into believing she owns their land.

With her marriage over, Lucy was glad to get away from Hollywood. She, Lucie, Desi Jr., and DeDe moved into a fancy apartment on the east side of Manhattan. It took four huge moving vans full of furniture, clothing, rugs, paintings, and toys to move Lucy to New York.

Lucy was still not much of a singer or a dancer. She was nearly fifty and had spent much of her career acting on a sitcom. It was not easy to perform in eight live shows a week, especially a musical. Lucy threw herself into voice and dance lessons.

Wildcat opened to the biggest advance sales in the history of the Alvin Theater. Opening night was on December 16, 1960. Desi was in the audience. The show was a hit. But it was too hard for Lucy to perform in the show for very long. Less than six months later, she returned to California with her children.

But they weren't alone. Lucy was now dating Gary Morton. He was a comedian she had met in New York. On November 19, 1961, Lucy and Gary got married. Although they tried to keep the wedding secret, a huge crowd gathered outside the Marble Collegiate church to wish them well.

Lucy couldn't wait to return to TV. Without Desi, Lucy would be the only star in her new show, *The Lucy Show.* Lucy played a widow named Lucy who had a son and a daughter.

Her best friend, Viv, was once again being played by the actress Vivian Vance, who had played Ethel Mertz on *I Love Lucy*. The day the show started shooting, Desi came by to wish Lucy luck.

He even gave her a four-leaf-clover charm made of emerald jade.

The Lucy Show premiered on October 1, 1962. It was an immediate hit. Everyone was thrilled that Lucy was back on TV.

Just one month later, Lucy bought Desi's share of their company and became the president of Desilu. She was the first woman in history to run a major production company. In the past she'd left the business side of things up to Desi. Now it was time to do things her way.

CHAPTER 8
Changing Times

The Lucy Show continued to be a hit with audiences. Lucy's new husband, Gary, was given the job of telling jokes to put the audience in a good mood before *The Lucy Show* was taped.

He had won over Lucie and Desi Jr. by being a good friend and encouraging their mother to be less strict. At this same time, Desi Jr. was moving into the spotlight himself. When he was twelve, he and two friends started a rock band.

Lucy wasn't sure how to deal with Desi Jr.'s surprise stardom. He was only thirteen and suddenly he was a big star. Lucy herself had worked for decades before she became famous. Desi Jr. loved to play drums, but he had always been a little shy. Having a famous mother hadn't prepared him for what it was like to be famous himself.

In July 1967, Lucy sold Desilu to Paramount for $17 million. It wasn't easy for Lucy to say good-bye to Desilu. She was proud of the company she had worked so hard at making a success. Lucy immediately started work on a new show, *Here's Lucy*. By this time, people had lost interest in fifteen-year-old Desi Jr.'s band. He and his sister,

Lucie, began acting on the new show, playing Lucy's children. Desi took out full-page ads in the newspapers congratulating his children on their TV debut. The ads also said "That red-headed gal playing your mother is the greatest."

Dino, Desi & Billy

Desi Arnaz Jr. became friends with Dino Martin and Billy Hinsche in elementary school. Dino's father, Dean Martin, was a famous singer and actor. Through him the boys met Frank Sinatra, another very famous singer and actor who gave them a recording contract.

The band, Dino, Desi & Billy, formed in 1964. They had two hit songs in 1965, "I'm a Fool" and "Not the Lovin' Kind." Although they continued to make records together until 1969, Billy Hinsche was the only member of the group who grew up to become a professional musician and vocalist.

Lucy still worked just as hard as she ever had. And she expected her children to work hard, too. Both Lucie and Desi Jr. were grateful for the weekends when they could relax with their father. In 1971, Desi Jr. left the show. He was seventeen.

In January 1972, Lucy fell and broke her leg while on a skiing trip. She spent almost the entire fifth season of *Here's Lucy* in a cast. The ratings on her show were falling. By early 1973, she was well enough to star in the movie version of the Broadway musical *Mame*.

Lucy's costar in the movie was Bea Arthur—a Broadway star who had her own television show called *Maude*. *Maude* was a very modern show that reflected more realistically how life was in the 1970s.

Bea Arthur

Sitcoms in the Seventies

Television once tried to show perfect families in perfect homes. But by the beginning of the 1970s, sitcoms were no longer afraid to deal with tougher issues. They showed working-class families in real-life situations. Their characters discussed war, racism, and women's issues. Compared to new shows like *The Mary Tyler Moore Show, M*A*S*H, All in the Family, Good Times,* and *Maude,* shows like *Here's Lucy* seemed very old-fashioned.

The new, down-to-earth sitcoms were nothing like *Here's Lucy*, which had by then dropped out of the top-twenty most-watched shows. The last episode of *Here's Lucy* aired in March of 1974. Lucy had spent the past twenty years playing Lucy. People wondered: Could she really retire?

CHAPTER 9
Queen of Comedy

In 1976, Lucy and Desi appeared together on a CBS special that celebrated the twenty-fifth anniversary of *I Love Lucy*. Even though it had stopped running years earlier, reruns of the show were still watched by millions of people every day in the United States. A new generation of fans had come to love it. *I Love Lucy* had been translated and dubbed into over a dozen languages and was popular all over the world. There were many places where Lucille Ball herself had never been but was loved just the same.

In the anniversary show, Lucy sang and danced. Other movie and TV stars appeared to introduce favorite scenes from *I Love Lucy* that everyone remembered. Even though television was changing in the 1970s, *I Love Lucy* seemed to be as funny as ever.

Although Desi and Lucy were no longer married, they were still good friends who loved each other. Their daughter, Lucie, was now married and had two children. Lucy and Desi had become grandparents.

Lucy loved her grandchildren, but she did not like being called "Grandma." She thought it made her sound old. She insisted on being called "Nana" instead. Lucy even got a new apartment in New York City so she could go to visit Lucie and her family there.

In April 1984, Lucy was honored by the Museum of Broadcasting as the "Queen of Television." For five months, the

museum showed hours of television shows and movies starring Lucy. She came to New York for the opening night of the show, called "Lucille Ball: First Lady of Comedy."

Lucy had not had a regular show in years, but people hadn't forgotten her.

Later that year, Lucy surprised everyone by appearing in a TV movie unlike anything she'd done before. *Stone Pillow* was the story of a homeless woman named Florabelle. The writer of the script used the name in honor of Lucy's grandmother. The movie showed that Lucy could still surprise people. For years she had only done comedy, but her role in *Stone Pillow* was a serious one.

Not long after the success of *Stone Pillow*, Desi was admitted to the hospital. He had lung cancer. Lucy wanted to visit him, but he refused. Desi didn't want her to see him looking so sick. But Lucy finally insisted on getting into the hospital, and the two spent a long afternoon together. Three weeks later, Desi Arnaz died in his daughter Lucie's arms.

Many reporters asked Lucy how she felt about Desi's death. She told them how she and Desi had stayed close through all the years. She was happy that he was no longer sick but would miss him always. At the memorial service for Desi, Lucy cried the entire time.

After Desi's death, Lucy didn't appear on television very often. In 1988 her old friend Bob Hope invited her to celebrate his eighty-fifth birthday on a TV special. Shortly after the show, she collapsed. She'd had a minor heart attack and a stroke that left her partially paralyzed. She had trouble using the right side of her body. It was hard for her to speak or eat. Lucy worked with a physical therapist to get better. In three months she was walking again and she could speak more clearly. By November 1988, she was well enough to appear on one of her favorite game shows, *Super Password*.

Bob Hope (1903–2003)

Born Leslie Townes Hope in Eltham, England, Bob Hope became a comedy star in American vaudeville. He went on to appear in many films and to host the Academy Awards more times than anyone else. He also made many popular comedy specials for TV. His show-business career lasted nearly eighty years, during which he made fifty-seven tours for the USO—United Service Organizations—to entertain Americans in the military.

The following February she was invited to appear with Bob Hope at the 1989 Academy Awards. She wore a black beaded gown with a gold sequined collar. The skirt was slit up one side.

Lucy was still proud of the long legs that had once gotten her a job as a Chesterfield Girl. She and Bob Hope got a standing ovation when they appeared.

Hope invited Lucy to come to Paris with him to be in his next TV special.

But three weeks after the awards, Lucy had another heart attack. She was rushed to the hospital. Letters poured in from across the country. The hospital received five thousand phone calls from around the world. The shopping mall across the street from the hospital hung a huge banner out front that read "We Love Lucy!"

On April 26, 1989, Lucy had yet another heart attack and died.

On the following Monday, May 8, many people around the country shared a moment of silence at 9:00 p.m.—*I Love Lucy*'s old timeslot.

Lucille Ball was a television pioneer. Reruns and internet clips of *I Love Lucy*, *The Lucy Show*, and *Here's Lucy* still make people laugh just as much as they did in past decades. The shows have been seen in eighty countries and twenty-one languages, including Japanese and Russian. She wasn't a beauty queen or even a highly trained actress. So Lucy invented a role that worked best for her: a television wife and mother who just happened to also be named Lucy. And in doing so, the Queen of Comedy had captured the hearts of people everywhere.

Timeline of Lucille Ball's Life

1911	— Lucille Desiree Ball is born in Jamestown, New York
1933	— Moves to Hollywood
1940	— Meets and marries Desi Arnaz.
1944	— Grandfather Fred Hunt dies
1950	— Founds Desilu productions with Desi
1951	— *I Love Lucy* premieres
1953	— Desi Arnaz Jr. and his TV counterpart, Little Ricky Ricardo, are born
1960	— Appears in last episode of the *Lucy-Desi Comedy Hour*
	— Divorces Desi Arnaz
1961	— Marries Gary Morton
1962	— *The Lucy Show* premieres
1965	— Appears on TV in color for the first time
1968	— *Here's Lucy* premieres
1974	— Stars in the movie *Mame*
1986	— Desi Arnaz dies
1989	— Dies in Los Angeles, California

Timeline of the World

1911	RMS *Titanic* is launched in Belfast
1920	Prohibition of alcohol begins in the United States
1924	King Tut's tomb opened in Egypt
1931	Alka Seltzer introduced
1937	Daffy Duck debuts in cartoon short *Porky's Duck Hunt*
1945	Ho Chi Minh elected president of North Vietnam
1949	FBI's "10 Most Wanted" fugitive program begins
1955	Cellist Yo-Yo Ma born in France
1960	Two Russian dogs become the first living animals to return from space
1966	Cultural Revolution begins in China
1972	Kareem Abdul-Jabbar named NBA MVP
1979	Susan B. Anthony becomes the first woman to appear on a US coin
1981	MTV, a TV channel showing only music videos, premieres
1985	First public mobile phone call is placed in the United Kingdom by Ernie Wise
1989	Chinese students protesting for democracy attacked in Tiananmen Square, Beijing, China

Bibliography

Ball, Lucille. *Love, Lucy*. New York: Putnam, 1996.

Ceplair, Larry, and Steven Englund. *The Inquisition in Hollywood: Politics in the Film Community, 1930–1960*. Garden City, NY: Anchor Press, 1980.

Flint, Peter B. "Lucille Ball, Spirited Doyenne of TV Comedies, Dies at 77." *New York Times*. April 27, 1989.

Harris, Warren G. *Lucy & Desi: the Legendary Love Story of Television's Most Famous Couple*. New York: Simon & Schuster, 1991.

Morella, Joe, and Edward Z. Epstein. *Lucy: the Bittersweet Life of Lucille Ball*. Secaucus, NJ: Lyle Stuart, 1973.

Pinkerton, Jonathan. "100 facts about Lucille Ball celebrating what would
  have been her 100th birthday." *Examiner*. http://www.examiner.com/
  article/100-facts-about-lucille-ball-celebrating-what-would-have-
  been-her-100th-birthday.

Sanders, Coyne Steven, and Tom Gilbert. *Desilu: The Story of Lucille Ball
  and Desi Arnaz*. New York: Morrow, 1993.

Schindehette, Susan. "The Real Story of Desi and Lucy." *People Magazine*.
  February 18, 1991.